W9-DCV-408

WHAT IT MEANS TO BE
SERIES

PUBLISHER	Joseph R. DeVarennes
PUBLICATION DIRECTOR	Kenneth H. Pearson
ADVISORS	Roger Aubin Robert Furlonger
EDITORIAL MANAGER	Jocelyn Smyth
EDITORS	Ann Martin Shelley McGuinness Robin Rivers Mayta Tannenbaum
ARTISTS	Richard Comely Greg Elliott Summer Morse Barbara Pileggi Steve Pileggi Mike Stearns
PRODUCTION MANAGER	Ernest Homewood
PRODUCTION ASSISTANTS	Catherine Gordon Kathy Kishimoto
PUBLICATION ADMINISTRATOR	Anna Good

Canadian Cataloguing in Publication Data

La Grange, Michelle
   What it means to be—fair

(What it means to be; 23)
ISBN 0-7172-2238-1

1. Fairness — Juvenile literature.
I. Pileggi, Steve.   II. Title.   III. Title: Fair.   IV. Series.

BJ1533.F2L32   1987   j177'.5   C87-095066-5

Copyright © 1987 by Grolier Limited. All rights reserved.

WHAT IT MEANS TO BE ...

FAIR

Written by
Michelle La Grange

Illustrated by
Steve Pileggi

Fair people include others in activities.

Mitchell, Tammy and Hannah were giggling in the play corner of their classroom.

"I love playing Let's Pretend," said Hannah. "Why don't we put on these dress-up clothes and play Farmer?"

"Good idea! I'll put on these overalls and milk the cows." Mitchell wriggled into his costume.

"And I'll put on this farmer's cap and brush the horses," added Tammy, rummaging through the clothes trunk.

Hannah said, "I'm going to use this bucket and feed the chickens." As she looked up, she noticed Janice standing alone, watching them with a sad expression on her face.

"Janice, would you like to play with us? You can drive the tractor," Hannah offered.

Janice grinned. "Gee, thanks. I wasn't sure if there was room for me."

Hannah smiled. "There's always room for you."

Leaving people out of a group can make them feel unhappy. If you ask others to share in your activities, everyone feels good.

Being fair means letting others share in decisions.

"That was really fun," said Tammy, sinking back into a big beanbag chair. "Do you guys want to play another game? I think there's still enough time before reading period."

"How about Duck, Duck, Goose?" asked Hannah.

"I'd rather play Wonderball Goes Round and Round," said Mitchell.

"So would I," said Janice. "What about you, Tammy?"

"I like Duck, Duck, Goose better. So it looks like half of us want to play one thing and the other half want to play something else. What should we do?"

"Since Hannah suggested an idea first, let's do that for a while," said Janice. "And if we have time we'll play Wonderball too. Otherwise we can play it tomorrow."

Everyone nodded in agreement.

It is best to consider everyone's opinion when you are trying to decide on a group activity. That way a fair choice can be made.

Fair people do not jump to conclusions.

Ryan gazed out the family room window and watched as the wind bent trees nearly in half and the rain flooded the flower garden.

"I hate thunder and lightning," said Ryan as he hugged his pet rabbit, Hoppy. Hoppy squirmed in his arms.

"Don't be a baby, Ryan. There's nothing to be afraid of," his brother Cameron scoffed, adding another card to the card house he was building. "This house sure is big, isn't it?"

"It sure is," agreed Ryan. He was glad to have something else to think about instead of the thunder.

"I'm going to find another deck of cards to make the house even taller. Don't touch it while I'm gone, Ryan, or it'll fall down," Cameron warned.

"I won't," Ryan answered.

Just then, a loud clap of thunder rang through the house. Before Ryan could stop him, Hoppy leaped from his arms onto Cameron's card house. It collapsed in an instant and Hoppy ran under the chesterfield.

A moment later, Cameron walked into the room. "Look what you did!" he roared. "I told you not to touch my card house, but you had to fool around with it, didn't you!"

"That's not what happened," cried Ryan, emerging from beneath the chesterfield with Hoppy in his arms. "The thunder scared Hoppy and he jumped on it. He moved too fast for me to stop him, Cameron. It was an accident."

"Oh," Cameron replied, feeling a little ashamed. "I guess I should have asked you what happened. I'm sorry I yelled at you, Ryan."

"That's okay, Cameron," replied Ryan. "Hey, why don't we build a new card house together?" The brothers set out to build the tallest card house ever.

Always give someone a chance to explain what happened. Otherwise, you might jump to the wrong conclusion and hurt someone's feelings.

Fair people always share.

Kim stumbled into her house through the back door and deposited a mountain of library books on the kitchen table.

"I'm starving," she said, heading straight for the refrigerator. "There's an apple and an orange. I think I'll have the orange."

Her brother Lee was sitting in a playpen in the kitchen. When he saw the orange in Kim's hand he reached toward it.

"You want an orange too?" she asked. "There's only one." As she peeled it and started eating it, he looked at her sadly.

"You're right," Kim said. "I should share this with you."

She smiled and gave him half the orange—one segment at a time. Lee grinned up at her.

It is only fair to share when more than one person wants the same thing.

Being fair means giving everyone a chance.

Jason and Janice were playing in their front yard when Paul arrived. He was excited and out of breath from running.

"Look at the new ball and bat that my grandma gave me. Want to come play with me in the park?"

"Sure. I'll just tell my mom where we are going," Jason answered, and ran into the house.

Half a minute later he ran back out. "She said we can go. Come on, Janice."

At the park, Paul said, "Jason, you can throw, I'll bat and Janice can run after the ball when I hit it."

"Okay," agreed Jason. He threw the ball. Paul swung hard and hit the ball far into the field. Janice hurried after it as fast as her legs would take her. When she got it, she started running toward Jason to give the ball back.

"No, no, silly," Paul yelled. "Just throw it back!"

Janice stopped and tried to throw it, but the ball fell far away from Jason.

"That's okay, Janice," said Jason. "Maybe you would like to bat instead."

Janice looked at Paul. "Can I try?" she asked timidly.

"It's probably too heavy for you," Paul grumbled as he handed her the bat.

Jason showed her how to hold the bat and then threw her the ball. Janice swung with all her might and missed.

"You don't know how to do anything," Paul sneered. "You're too little to play with us."

Tears came to Janice's eyes.

"Come on, Paul," said Jason. "Everyone has to learn and the only way to do that is to try."

"You're right. I'm sorry, Janice," Paul apologized. "Try hitting the ball again."

With Paul's help, Janice started to play better and the three of them had such a good time that they agreed to play again soon.

If you are fair, you will be patient and give others a chance to learn. Everyone will benefit.

Fair people do not play favorites.

Cameron said he would be the umpire for the Saturday afternoon baseball games at the neighborhood park. Ryan and his friends were excited. It made them feel like grown-up players to have an umpire. Ryan was secretly pleased because he thought Cameron would be easier on him than anyone else and that his team would win for sure.

It was a bright sunny day when they all headed down to the playground. They practiced throwing and catching before they divided into teams. Ryan was chosen as the captain of one team with Colette pitching. Kim was the captain of the other team and Dylan was the pitcher. Cameron took his place behind the catcher.

Both teams played hard but soon Kim's team was ahead. Ryan couldn't understand it. Cameron didn't seem to be giving his team a break at all.

Kim's team won the game nine to five. Kim walked over to thank Cameron. "You were fair and square. I hope you'll be our umpire again."

"Any time," said Cameron.

As Cameron and Ryan walked home, Ryan dragged his feet.

"You all played a good game," said Cameron. "I really enjoyed myself."

"Humph," muttered his brother. "At least you could have been easier on me."

"What do you mean?" asked Cameron.

"A few of the strikes you called could have passed for balls. And I was *almost* safe that time you called me out."

"You wouldn't want me to cheat, would you?" asked Cameron, looking surprised.

"Well, no. Not if you put it that way," admitted Ryan.

"The umpire's job is to be impartial and not to favor either team," Cameron explained. "That's what I did."

"I guess you're right," Ryan said. "Next time my team will just have to try harder."

If you are fair, you will treat people equally.

Fair people always play by the rules.

Colette, Tammy, Mitchell and Kim were all at the park, playing on the swings and monkey bars.

"Who wants to play hide-and-go-seek?" asked Colette.

"Me! Me! Me!" yelled the others.

"Great. Who will be It? Tammy, will you start?"

"Oh, all right," Tammy answered. "How high do I count?"

"Count to twenty," said Kim. "Stand by this tree, hide your eyes and count slowly. Remember, no peeking."

Tammy walked to the tree, hid her eyes and began to count loudly, "One . . . two . . . three . . ."

All the kids ran in circles, looking for a place to hide. They tried not to laugh in case Tammy heard them and discovered their hiding places.

Everyone found a hiding place quickly except Mitchell. All his favorite places were taken. He glanced at Tammy.

"Sixteen . . . seventeen . . . eighteen," she called. But now, instead of hiding her eyes, she was searching the playground. She saw Mitchell dive behind a fence.

"Nineteen . . . twenty. Ready or not, here I come. Mitchell, I saw you! You're behind the fence. You're It," Tammy called, and she tagged the tree.

"No fair," cried Mitchell. "I saw you peeking. It's not any fun if you won't play by the rules. I'm going home." He started to walk away.

"Wait," called Tammy. "I'm sorry I peeked, Mitchell. Please stay. If I cover my eyes and count to ten, will you find another hiding place?"

"Okay," said Mitchell. "And *this* time," he added with his eyes twinkling, "I'll be hidden so well that I'll be the last one that you find."

Everyone likes to win and you may sometimes be tempted to cheat "just a little." If you stop to think how you would feel about someone else who cheated, you will do the fair thing and follow the rules.

It is only fair to share the work as well as the fun.

Kim and Colette were walking home together after school. "What a fun day," said Kim. "All that work has made me as hungry as a bear." She let out a deep growl. "Let's go to my house for a snack."

The two girls scampered off to Kim's house.

Once they were in the kitchen, Kim asked, "Do you like peanut butter and honey sandwiches?"

"They're my favorite," Colette answered.

Kim spread the peanut butter and honey so thickly that it drizzled off the edges of the sandwich, leaving sticky spots all over the table.

"Yum! That was delicious," said Colette after they had finished eating. "Let's go play."

Kim looked at the messy table. "I'd better clean up first," she sighed.

"I'll help you," volunteered Colette. Within minutes the kitchen was sparkling and there was no sign of honey anywhere.

If you are fair, you will help clean up any mess you had a share in making—even when no one will hold you responsible.

Being fair means considering other people's feelings.

Bobby and Joey were playing at Bobby's house one day. Joey had just gotten a bright new shirt and Bobby couldn't resist teasing him.

"Stand back! I need sunglasses to shield my eyes from the color," he joked.

Joey smiled and continued working on the puzzle.

"The airport could use you as a beacon for planes landing at night," said Bobby, laughing louder.

"That's not very funny," replied Joey. His face was red. When Bobby just kept on laughing, Joey got up and left without saying goodbye.

Bobby's father came in. "Why did Joey leave? I thought he was staying for dinner."

"I don't know. I was only teasing him about his new shirt."

"Do you think you might have hurt his feelings?" asked his dad.

Bobby thought for a moment. "I guess . . ."

"Do you think you should go talk to him?" suggested his dad.

"No, he'll get over it by tomorrow."

"Are you sure?"

"Of course," said Bobby.

But the next day at school Joey didn't want to play with Bobby. He didn't even sit by him during art class. After school Bobby found Joey hitting a tennis ball against a wall.

"Are you mad at me?" asked Bobby.

"Sort of," mumbled Joey.

"I was just trying to be funny yesterday. I guess I went too far, huh?"

Joey nodded his head. "Think how you would have felt if I'd done that to you."

"I'm sorry," said Bobby. "Do you want to finish the puzzle at my house?"

"Okay," Joey replied.

Sometimes you may forget to think of your friends' feelings. Remember to treat your friends the way you want to be treated.

Being fair means taking turns.

Hannah and Mitchell were playing on the merry-go-round at the park. They took turns pushing each other on the spinning platform. Soon they were out of breath and feeling dizzy. They collapsed on the grass giggling loudly.

When they caught their breath Hannah asked, "What do you want to do now?"

"Well, we've already been on the slide and the teeter-totters, and we've played in the sandbox. What about the swings?" suggested Mitchell.

"Okay," said Hannah.

They ran over to the swings. Some other kids were already there, and only one swing was free.

"You go ahead, Mitchell," said Hannah.

"Thanks, Hannah. I'll give you a turn in a minute."

They shared the swing until another one was free.

Sometimes you may not want to share playground equipment or toys. If you are fair, you let others have a turn so everyone can have fun.

Fair people are honest.

Brrring! The bell rang loudly to tell all the kids that another school day was over. Paul and Dylan burst through the wide school doors. "I'll race you to the sidewalk," Paul called to Dylan. The two boys took off as fast as lightning and reached the sidewalk at the same time.

"Stop for a minute . . . I need to catch my breath," Paul said panting. As the two rested, Paul spotted a soccer ball in the nearby ditch.

"Hey! Look what I found, Dylan!" he exclaimed, running over to pick up the ball. "I've always wanted a soccer ball and now I have one."

"Don't you think we should find out who it belongs to?" asked Dylan.

"No way! Finders keepers, losers weepers. I found it, so it's mine," Paul said stubbornly.

"I don't know, Paul. If that were your ball and you lost it, wouldn't you want someone to give it back to you?"

"Well . . . I guess so," Paul said uncertainly.

"Let's see if it has anyone's name on it," Dylan said. They turned the ball over and saw a name.

"E-v-a . . . Eva," they said together.

"She lives near me," said Dylan. "Let's go take it to her."

The two boys hurried to Eva's house and knocked on the door. Eva answered. When she saw Dylan and Paul with her new soccer ball, she whooped with joy.

"You found it! Thank you so much. I was so upset when I lost it. I'm really happy now!"

"No problem," said Paul, smiling at Dylan. "We're glad that we could help you."

If you are fair, you will do the honest thing. Then you will feel good about yourself and others will feel good about you too.

It can be fair to treat people differently due to special circumstances.

Eva was playing table tennis with Joey. She had never played before so it took her a while to understand the rules and learn how to hit the ball properly.

"You're getting there," approved Joey.

Just then they heard a knock at the door. It was Jason and Colette. "Can we play too?" asked Jason.

"Sure. We can teach Eva to play doubles. She's just learning how to play," explained Joey.

"I'll be your partner, Joey," said Jason. He liked winning and he knew Joey was the best player there.

"I think Joey and Eva should be partners," suggested Colette. "That way the newest player and the one with the most practice will be together."

"Why should Eva get special treatment?" grumbled Jason.

"This is the first time she's ever played table tennis," said Joey. "Don't you remember how long it took you to become a good player?"

"Yeah, you're right," muttered Jason.

The four friends started playing doubles. Eva made some mistakes, especially when she got excited. Joey helped and encouraged her. Pretty soon Jason started to enjoy himself. The two teams were fairly evenly matched and the game ended up as a tie.

"You're getting really good, Eva," said Jason. "Maybe next time you can be my partner."

"I'd like that," Eva replied.

There are certain times when someone needs to be treated differently due to age, experience or other special reasons. You can help by offering encouragement and not drawing attention to the special treatment. If you are fair, you are honest and considerate. Here are some other ways to be fair:

- Include others in your activities.
- Take turns.
- Listen to other people's views.
- Share your things.

Printed and bound in U.S.A.